W9-AVL-997

People Around Town

MEET THE POLICEMAN

By Joyce Jeffries

Gareth Stevens
Publishing

RAP 8597413

Please visit our website, www.garethstevens.com. For a free color catalog of all our high-quality books, call toll free 1-800-542-2595 or fax 1-877-542-2596.

Library of Congress Cataloging-in-Publication Data

Jeffries, Joyce.
  Meet the policeman / Joyce Jeffries.
    p. cm. — (People around town)
  Includes index.
  ISBN 978-1-4339-7337-6 (pbk.)
  ISBN 978-1-4339-7338-3 (6-pack)
  ISBN 978-1-4339-7336-9 (library binding) —
  1. Police—Juvenile literature. I. Title.
  HV7922.J44 2013
  363.2—dc23

                              201200830

First Edition

Published in 2013 by
Gareth Stevens Publishing
111 East 14th Street, Suite 349
New York, NY 10003

Editor: Katie Kawa
Designer: Andrea Davison-Bartolotta

Photo credits: Cover Creatas/Thinkstock; p. 1 Stockbyte/Thinkstock; p. 5 Photodisc/Thinkstock; p. 7 John Roman Images/Shutterstock.com; p. 9 Kanwarjit Singh Boparai/Shutterstock.com; pp. 11, 24 (radar gun) VladKol/Shutterstock.com; p. 13 Lisa F. Young/Shutterstock.com; p. 15 Carolina K. Smith, M. D./Shutterstock.com; p. 17 Dwight Smith/Shutterstock.com; pp. 19, 24 (uniform) Lifesize/Thinkstock; p. 21 Bill Pugliano/Stringer/Getty Images; pp. 23, 24 (mounted police) Stuart Monk/Shutterstock.com.

Printed in the United States of America

CPSIA compliance information: Batch #CS12GS: For further information contact Gareth Stevens, New York, New York at 1-800-542-2595.

Contents

A policeman's job is
to keep people safe.

He is very brave!

He makes sure people follow laws. These are important rules.

He uses a tool to see
how fast cars go.
It is a radar gun.

He stops cars
that go too fast.

He has a special car. It has red and blue lights.

15

The car makes
a loud noise.
This is called a siren.

Policemen wear special clothes. This is called a uniform.

Some work with dogs.
These are K9 teams.

Mounted police ride
on horses!

23

Words to Know

mounted
police

radar
gun

uniform

Index